Countries Around the World

Egypt

Marta Segal Block

www.raintreepublishers.co.uk
Visit our website to find out more information about Raintree books.

To order:
☎ Phone 0845 6044371
🖷 Fax +44 (0) 1865 312263
✉ Email myorders@raintreepublishers.co.uk

Customers from outside the UK please telephone +44 1865 312262

Raintree is an imprint of Capstone Global Library Limited, a company incorporated in England and Wales having its registered office at 7 Pilgrim Street, London, EC4V 6LB – Registered company number: 6695582

Text © Capstone Global Library Limited 2012
First published in hardback in 2012
The moral rights of the proprietor have been asserted.

Edited by Abby Colich and Megan Cotugno
Designed by Philippa Jenkins
Original illustrations © Capstone Global Library Ltd.
Illustrated by Oxford Designers & Illustrators
Picture research by Liz Alexander
Originated by Capstone Global Library Ltd.
Printed in China by CTPS

ISBN 978 1 406 23562 3 (hardback)
16 15 14 13 12
10 9 8 7 6 5 4 3 2 1

British Library Cataloguing in Publication Data
Block, Marta Segal.
 Egypt. -- (Countries around the world)
 1. Egypt--Juvenile literature.
 I. Title II. Series
 962'.055-dc22

Acknowledgements
We would like to thank the following for permission to reproduce photographs: The Art Archive: pp. 8 (Collection Antonovich / Gianni Dagli Orti), 10 (Musée du Château de Versailles / Gianni Dagli Orti); Corbis: pp. 20 (© Goran Tomasevic/Reuters), 24 (© Tara Todras-Whitehill/Reuters), 29 (© Lynsey Addario/VII Network), 34 (© epa); Dreamstime.com: p. 25 (© Markwaters); Getty Images: pp. 7 (Ethan Miller), 12-13: (Hulton Archive), 17 (AFP), 28 (David Silverman), 30 (Cris Bouroncle/AFP), 36 (Misam Saleh/AFP); Photolibrary: pp. 11 (Steve Vidler), 19 (Henryk T Kaiser); Photoshot: p. 31 (Peter Schickert); Shutterstock: pp. 5 (© bumihills), 21 (© Peter Zaharov), 22 (© Roger De Marfa), 23 (© Uryadnikov Sergey), 27 (© Baloncici), 32 (© Louise Cukrov), 33(© CWB), 35 (© Brandelet), 37 (© Bzzuspajk), 46 (© Sportnet).

Cover photograph of Bazaar at Khan Al-Khalili, Cairo, Egypt, reproduced with permission from Photolibrary (Radius Images).

We would like to thank Shiera S. el-Malik for her invaluable help in the preparation of this book.

Every effort has been made to contact copyright holders of material reproduced in this book. Any omissions will be rectified in subsequent printings if notice is given to the publisher.

Contents

Some words are printed in bold, **like this**. You can find out what they mean by looking in the glossary.

Introducing Egypt

When many people think of Egypt, they think of things like mummies, pyramids, **hieroglyphics**, the Sphinx, **Pharaohs**, King Tut, and the river Nile.

These are all important parts of this ancient country, but the country is also so much more. Egypt's river Nile has fed people for centuries, providing **papyrus**, the world's first paper, and also the first agriculture. Built in 1970, the Aswan **Dam** remains an important yet controversial engineering feat.

Languages of Egypt

The official name of Egypt is the Arab **Republic** of Egypt. In Arabic it is called *Jumhuriyat Misr al-Arabiyah* or *Misr* for short. Although English, French, and German are widely spoken in Egypt, Arabic is the official language. Many Egyptians also speak a language known as "Egyptian Arabic".

Egypt is very important politically. It was the first Arab country to make peace with neighbouring Israel. This makes Egypt a valuable friend to countries throughout the world.

Visiting Egypt

Located in northern Africa, Egypt covers an area of 995,450 square kilometres (384,345 square miles). Tourism is the country's largest source of foreign money. For centuries people have flocked to this country to see the pyramids and other ancient artifacts.

How to say...

Salaam is the Arabic word for "peace". It is often used as a greeting.

The river Nile has always been essential to Egypt's growth.

History: the land of the Pharaohs

The river Nile has drawn people to Egypt for centuries. Over 8,000 years ago, hunters and fishers first settled nearby. As they learned to work with the Nile and its regular patterns of flooding and **drought**, they began to grow certain kinds of grain. Later, they also kept animals.

The river Nile allowed people to travel to other parts of Africa, trading and bringing back new ideas. By 3000 BC, the Nile people were their own **civilization**. The ancient Egyptians also had their own written language, known as **hieroglyphics**.

	B		soft G, J		hard T, H	
	K		H		soft T, H	
	S		L		long E	
	CH		M		soft T, H	
	SH		R		long U, OO	
	hard S, Z		N		long I short I hard Y	
	D		P		short A short E short O	
	F, V		QU		long A	
	hard G		T			

This chart shows some common hieroglyphics and their translations.

The Pharaohs

In about 3100 BC, two kingdoms known as Upper and Lower Egypt united under a powerful leader. This leader came to be known as a **Pharaoh**. The Pharaohs conquered new lands including Nubia (modern-day Sudan), Palestine (modern-day Israel), and Syria.

Although it was unusual in the ancient world, Egyptian women could inherit and own property, and even ask for a divorce. Women could even become Pharaohs. The earliest female Pharaoh was Meryt-Neith. She was possibly the third Pharaoh and ruled for almost three years. The longest ruling female Pharaoh was Hatshepsut. While the exact years of her rule are difficult to determine, she had power for over 15 years. Portraits of Hatshepsut almost always show her as a man with a traditional beard.

King Tut (Tutankhamen) is the Pharaoh most famous today, but most historians believe he was a fairly unimportant ruler in his own time.

Alexander the Great

In 332 BC, Alexander the Great of Macedonia conquered Egypt. Macedonia is near Greece in Europe – not very close to Egypt. Alexander founded the Ptolemy **dynasty** of Pharaohs as well as the city of Alexandria, which he named after himself. Since its founding, Alexandria has been recognized as an important city for learning.

From Greece to Rome

The last Ptolemy Pharaoh was Queen Cleopatra. Cleopatra tried to attack the **Roman Empire**, but lost. In 31 BC, Egypt came under Roman rule. Over the next 300 years, Rome changed the Egyptian culture, making Christianity the official religion. The Egyptian Christians were known as Coptics, and many still live in Egypt today.

CLEOPATRA (69 BC–AD 30)

Cleopatra was a descendant of one of Alexander the Great's generals. She first ruled Egypt with her father and brothers, and later ruled Egypt alone. Although many of the Ptolemy rulers spoke only Greek, Cleopatra learned Egyptian and presented herself as an Egyptian goddess. Today, most people know more about Cleopatra's love life than they know about her as ruler. Cleopatra had children by both Julius Caesar and his general, Marc Antony. Some say her beauty influenced Antony's attempted takeover of Rome. The story of Cleopatra survives in many plays, books, and works of art. She is always portrayed as an amazingly beautiful woman.

Although some sources say Cleopatra was probably not so very beautiful, the legend of her as a great beauty survives today.

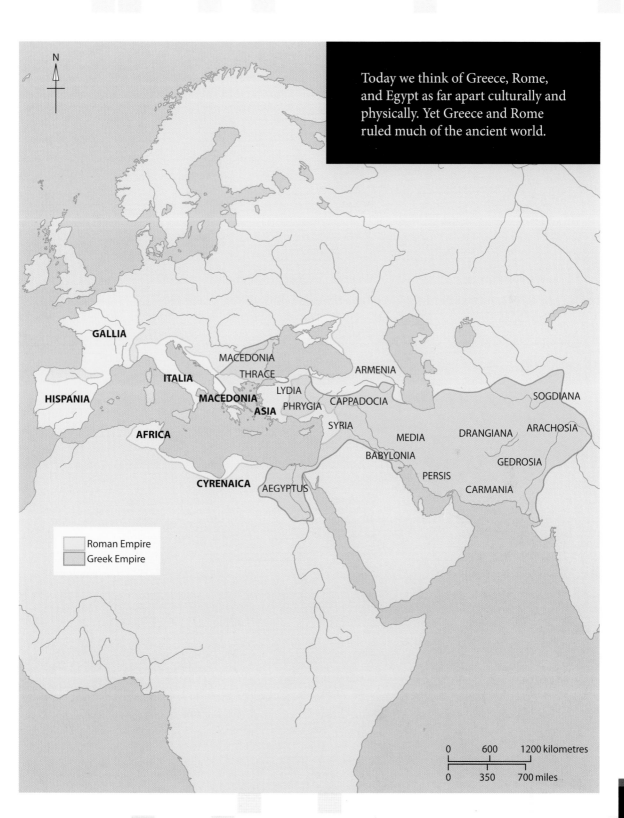

N

Today we think of Greece, Rome, and Egypt as far apart culturally and physically. Yet Greece and Rome ruled much of the ancient world.

GALLIA

MACEDONIA
THRACE
ITALIA
HISPANIA
MACEDONIA
LYDIA
ASIA
PHRYGIA
AFRICA

ARMENIA

SOGDIANA

CAPPADOCIA

SYRIA
MEDIA
BABYLONIA

DRANGIANA
ARACHOSIA

GEDROSIA

CYRENAICA
AEGYPTUS
PERSIS
CARMANIA

Roman Empire
Greek Empire

0   600   1200 kilometres

0   350   700 miles

Islam comes to Egypt

In AD 640, **Muslim** warriors from the Arabian **Peninsula** took over Egypt and founded the city that we know today as Cairo. **Islam** became the main religion of Egypt and remains so today. For over 200 years, Cairo was the centre of the Islamic Empire.

Napoleon and Egypt

In 1517 the Ottoman Empire, based in present-day Turkey, took over Egypt from a group of slave soldiers known as the **Mamluks**. The Mamluks eventually regained power in the 1700s. In 1798 **Napoleon Bonaparte** of France defeated the Mamluks and returned Egypt to the rule of the Ottoman Empire.

Napoleon and his troops assemble before the battle of the pyramids.

Napoleon wanted control of Egypt during the war between France and England. At the time, India was a British **colony** – and Egypt was part of a direct route from Britian to India. If France controlled Egypt, then the British would have more trouble travelling to their colony. After conquering Egypt, Napoleon brought Egyptian scholars and artists to France. Much of what we know about ancient Egypt comes from these scholars.

While in Egypt, French troops found the famous Rosetta Stone. The Rosetta Stone is a fragment of an ancient stone. On it is one message written in three ways: in hieroglyphics, in another form of Egyptian script, and in ancient Greek. The stone made it possible for scholars to **translate** ancient Egyptian hieroglyphics. Today the term "Rosetta Stone" often describes something that is a key to a mystery.

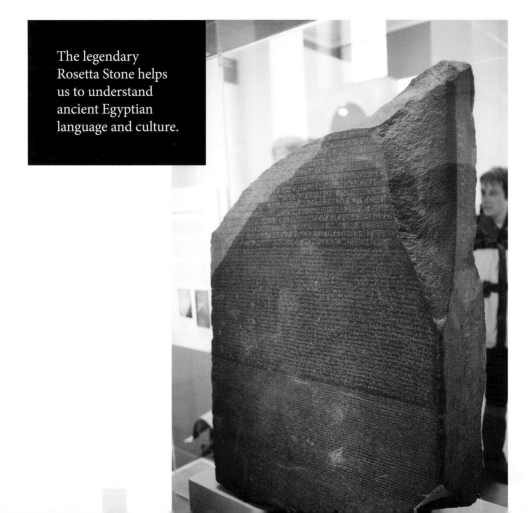

The legendary Rosetta Stone helps us to understand ancient Egyptian language and culture.

The Suez Canal

In 1859 Egypt and France built the Suez Canal. The canal is 160 kilometres (101 miles) long and links the Mediterranean Sea and the Red Sea. Before the canal was built, ships went around the tip of Africa to move goods between Asia and Europe. That one-way trip is 6,435 kilometres (4,000 miles)!

The Egyptian government sold its portion of the canal to Britain in 1869. In 1882 Britain invaded and took control of Egypt. Then, in 1914, Egypt became a British **protectorate**. Egypt regained some of its independence in 1922 but did not become fully independent for another 30 years.

Independence, war, and peace

In 1952 army officers took control of Egypt and declared it a **republic** with Colonel Gamal Abder Nasser as ruler. Nasser was very popular in the Arab world. Between 1954 and 2011, Egypt has only had three presidents: Nasser, Anwar Sadat, and Hosni Mubarak.

In February 2011, after a series of **riots**, Hosni Mubarak and his entire government were forced to **resign**. The riots were sparked by economic and political turmoil and inspired by a similar revolution in Tunisia. In return, the Egyptian revolution sparked revolutions in other Middle Eastern countries. There is currently an **interim** government.

The Suez Canal allowed traders to cut through Africa, saving time and increasing Europe's influence on Africa.

Regions and resources: the land of the Nile

Egypt has four main regions: the Nile Valley and Delta, the eastern region, the western region, and the Sinai **Peninsula**. Egypt is hot and dry all year. The greatest rainfall is in the north – but no more than 25 mm (one inch) per year – and the rain evaporates quickly in the hot sun. It is hottest in the south, near Aswan. Summer temperatures can rise to 50°C (122°F).

The Nile

The Nile region makes up only four per cent of Egypt's land; however, 99 per cent of Egyptians live there. The other one per cent is mostly **nomadic Bedouins**. Most of the economic activity in the country takes place in the Nile region. However, the Western Desert has large natural gas and oil **deposits** and offshore oil rigs operate in the Gulf of Suez.

Although tourism is Egypt's most important industry, turquoise, gold, and granite are mined, as are petroleum and natural gas. Corn, wheat, beans, fruits, and vegetables are grown. Farmers rear cattle, water buffalo, sheep, and goats.

How to say...

The ancient Egyptians called the Nile River *Aur* or *Ar*, which means black. Because of the rich, **fertile** soil in the river, the river water looks almost black. Yearly floods of the Nile deposit this dark soil on the banks, allowing Egyptians to grow crops. In modern Arabic, the Nile is called *Nahr an-Nil*.

Mediterranean Sea

ISRAEL

Damietta

Alexandria

Tanta

Abū Za'bal

Cairo

Suez

Hulwān

Al Bawīṭī

Al Minyā

Asyūṭ

Būr Safājah

Naj Hammādi

Qinā

Al Quṣayr

EGYPT

Luxor

Red Sea

Aswan

Lake Nasser

Abū Sunbul

LIBYA

SUDAN

N

Nile River

Petroleum refining

Chemicals (petrochemicals and fertilizers)

Heavy industry (automobile and military assembly)

Metal processing (steel and aluminum)

Cement

Textiles

Food processing

Tourism

Oil

Gas

Coal

Iron

Phosphate

Salt (marine)

0   250   500 kilometres
0   150   300 miles

This map shows the various types
of economic activity in Egypt. The
majority is located along the river Nile.

Aswan High Dam

The city of Aswan is situated on the river Nile's east **bank**. The stone quarries that provided stones for the ancient pyramids and other statues were located in Aswan.

In 1970 the Aswan High **Dam** was completed. It was thought that the dam would allow farmers to control the Nile and grow crops all year round. However, in addition to storing water, the dam also traps the rich soil of the Nile. This means that the Nile Valley is not as fertile as it used to be.

Pros and cons of the Aswan High Dam	
Pros	**Cons**
Two or three harvests each year, instead of only one	Dam traps soil, making Nile valley less rich and fertile
Drainage improved	Lower water levels caused collapse of parts of riverbanks
Lives and land saved, thanks to fewer floods	Farmers use too much water since water available year-round
Water available in both Egypt and Sudan in low-water years	Water quality not as good
Lake Nassar has increased fish population, providing important protein source	Increase in weeds because of change in water
High dam power station provides energy	Building of dam forced many people to move

The Aswan High Dam was built over a period of 12 years (1959–1970). Its completion was a great achievement, but also a source of controversy.

The Red Sea

East of the Nile is the Red Sea. No one is certain of the origin of the name "Red Sea". It might refer to the reddish **algae** in the water or to a bordering desert the ancient Egyptians called "Red Desert". The Red Sea is about 2,250 kilometres (1,398 miles) long.

The Sinai

Beyond the Red Sea is the Sinai Desert. Egypt's highest point is known as both Mount Catherine and Mount Sinai. It is 2,629 metres (8,625 feet) high. Because they are significant in the Bible, the Red Sea and Mount Sinai are both major tourist sites.

Western Desert

The Sahara Desert stretches across North Africa. Two thirds of Egypt's land is covered by the desert. This desert is sandy and harder to navigate than the Sinai Desert, but for centuries the nomadic Bedouin people moved across the desert. Today, many Bedouins have settled near the **oases** of the desert.

Mining

Petroleum and natural gas are Egypt's largest mineral resources. Petroleum makes up about one-third of Egypt's **exports**. The Arab Gas Pipeline opened in 2003. It carries natural gas from Egypt to Jordan.

Ancient Bedouins navigated the desert by following desert animals and watching the position of the stars.

Wildlife: honouring animals

The ancient Egyptians honoured animals. Many of their gods were part human and part animal, and animals were **mummified** after death just as people were. Snakes were feared, but also **revered** as gods. The ancient Egyptians reared animals such as cows and goats, and kept cats as pets. This was very unusual in ancient times.

Camels

Although camels are often seen as a symbol of Egypt and other desert countries, they are not native to the area. In 525 BC, Persia invaded Egypt and brought the first camels. These Persian camels were not well-suited for trading or travelling over the desert. It wasn't until the AD 640s that camels became common. The camel is often called the "ship of the desert" because it can carry people and goods.

Today camels are not used very often to cross the desert, but are used for tourist rides and to provide meat, milk, wool, and skins.

Camel racing is a popular sport in Egypt.

The hoopoe is one of the most distinctive Egyptian birds. It has black and white wings, a long bill that curves downward, and a large crest on its head.

Birds

There are more than 400 species of bird in Egypt. Many birds stop in Egypt as part of their **migration** from northern Europe to southern Africa for the winter. But other birds such as eagles and falcons live in the desert, and kingfishers, pelicans, and cranes live in and near the swamps and waters.

Marine wildlife

Because very little water enters the Red Sea from the Indian Ocean or from other bodies of water, the Red Sea has its own unique fish. Many of these fish are very colourful, including the various species of butterfly fish.

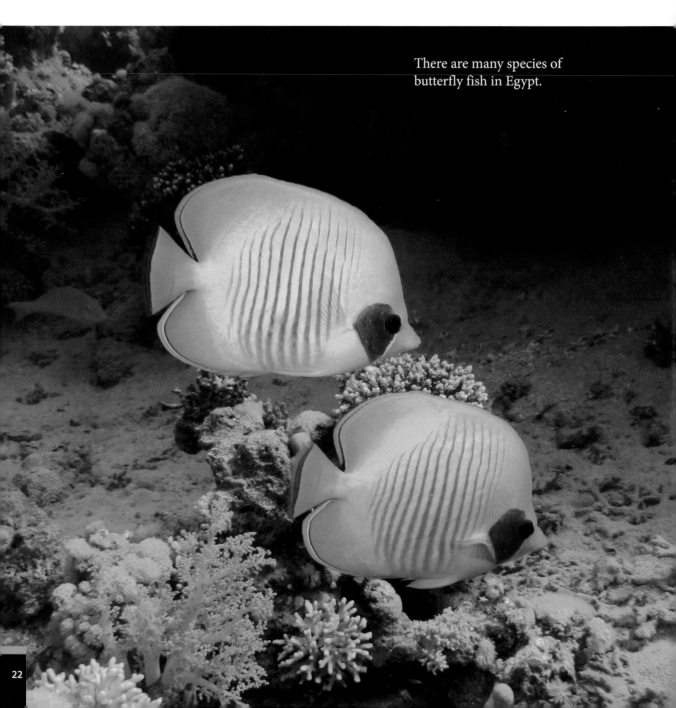

There are many species of butterfly fish in Egypt.

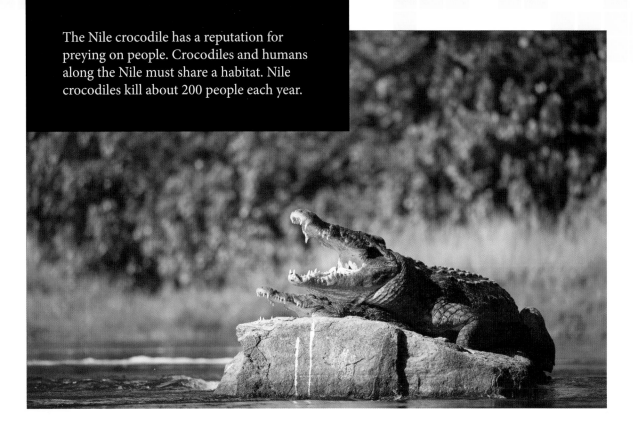

The Nile crocodile has a reputation for preying on people. Crocodiles and humans along the Nile must share a habitat. Nile crocodiles kill about 200 people each year.

Hundreds of years ago you could find hippopotamuses and lions along the **banks** of the Nile. Those animals are no longer present, but the Nile still bursts with life. Perhaps the most famous creature of the Nile is the **endangered** Nile crocodile. The Nile crocodile grows to be about 5 metres (16 feet) long and 227 kilograms (500 pounds) in weight. Mummified crocodiles and crocodile eggs have been discovered in ancient Egyptian tombs. This shows that the Egyptians thought the crocodiles were important.

Endangered species

Egypt has 21 regions where animals are protected. Regions include **oases**, deserts, mountains, coastal areas, and wetlands. But, because of shrinking deserts, many species in Egypt are losing their natural **habitats**. Endangered species include the sand cat, Nubian ibex (a type of wild goat), dalmation shark, and golden hamster. Birds and water animals are also endangered by man-made constructions such as the Aswan **Dam** and Suez Canal. Animals that have been endangered because of the dam and the canal include the white-headed duck, Nile crocodile, greater spotted eagle, Egyptian tortoise and cape shark.

Infrastructure: a government in transition

Officially, Egypt has been a **parliamentary democracy** for years. The government held regular elections and voting was **compulsory**, meaning everyone was required to vote. But in practice, Egypt was actually a **dictatorship**.

From 1981 to 2011, the government was led by Hosni Mubarak. There was only one **political party** and until 2005, only one person ever ran for president. In 2005, for the first time, rules were changed so that more than one person and party could run for president. However, the rules were so difficult to understand that most people did not think that the elections were fair.

The 2005 elections were the first Egyptian elections to have more than one political party.

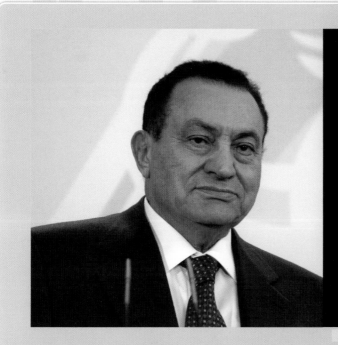

Hosni Mubarak was often on lists of the world's worst dictators. Other countries supported him because they saw other possible presidents as worse choices for Egypt and international peace.

HOSNI MUBARAK (B. 1928)

In 1981 Anwar Sadat was **assassinated**, and Hosni Mubarak became president. Mubarak had been Sadat's vice president, responsible for the country's day-to-day business. Many of Sadat's policies, including making peace with Israel, had been Mubarak's ideas. After Sadat's murder, Mubarak kept most of the policies in place. As Egypt's leader, Mubarak survived six assassination attempts, but his presidency could not survive the revolutionary fever that gripped Egypt in the early days of 2011.

Mubarak held on to power very tightly. He was often referred to as a **dictator** outside of Egypt. Mubarak was especially concerned about Islamists, or Islamic **fundamentalism**. Islamic fundamentalists want the country to be run according to ancient **Muslim** law (known as Sharia law). Islamists often resort to **terrorism** to try and influence politics.

In 2011 a revolution forced Mubarak out of power. Before leaving he attempted to make **concessions**, but by that time it was too late and the Egyptian people demanded that he leave.

The future government

What kind of government Egyptians will elect in the coming years is very unclear. Many people believe that the Egyptian people feel angry towards the United States and European powers for their past support of Mubarak. These people worry that Egyptians will elect a government that supports Muslim fundamentalism.

Egypt has always been an important Middle Eastern **ally** for Western powers. It is unclear what effect a government that is hostile to these powers will have on relationships.

Egypt's economy

The monetary unit of Egypt is known as the Egyptian Pound (EGP). The Nile Valley has always been the central economic force of Egypt. However, from 2004 to 2008 President Mubarak tried to create **reforms** that would attract foreign investors. Much of Egypt's current economy is dependent on tourism. The global economic crisis that began in 2009 has slowed Egypt's growth. Even during the best parts of Egypt's economic history, living conditions for most Egyptians have been poor.

Healthcare

Egypt's growing population is putting a strain on its healthcare system. As in many countries, healthcare is provided by a variety of groups, including government agencies and private organizations. Religious organizations are a growing provider of healthcare in the country.

Life expectancy in Egypt is 75 years for women and 70 years for men. The most common diseases in the country are those associated with living near water, including bacterial diahorreah, typhoid, Rift Valley fever, and schistosomiasis, a disease caused by a parasite.

As in many parts of the world, poor Egyptians do not always benefit from good economic conditions – and suffer during bad ones.

Education

For centuries, Alexandria was known as the centre of knowledge of the Ancient world. Egypt has a reputation as an educated country and has many universities, including Al-Azhar which was founded in AD 970.

Approximately 33 per cent of Egypt's population is under the age of 15, making education an important issue in the country. Over 71 per cent of the population can read. The government provides free education for 11 years, or up to university level. But in many families, children leave school at the age of 12 to help out with a family business or farm.

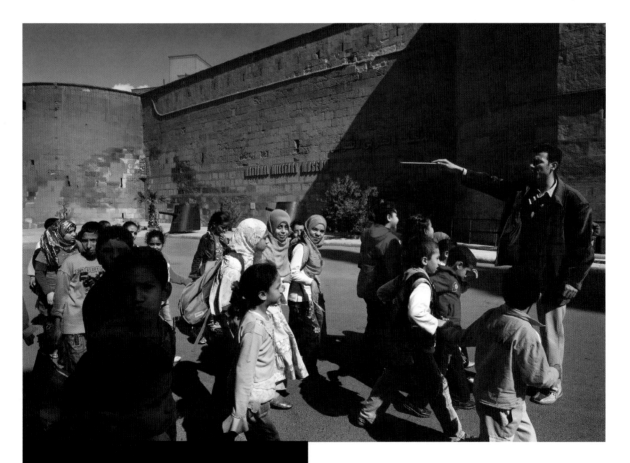

These Egyptian children are on a field trip to an Egyptian military museum.

In contrast to many other Islamic countries, girls in Egypt are encouraged to stay in school.

YOUNG PEOPLE

Boys and girls both go to school in Egypt, and the government urges girls to stay in school longer and delay having children. Children in Egypt study the same subjects as children in the UK.

Culture: the heart of Egypt

Islam is the official religion of Egypt. According to the constitution, all laws must agree with Islamic law. Yet, the constitution bans the existence of religious **political parties**. About 90 to 95 per cent of Egyptians are **Muslim**, but Egyptian Christians, known in Egypt as Coptics, are also an important part of society. In fact, Egyptian Muslims and Christians get along well. There is also a small number of Egyptians who are of Jewish or Baha'i faith.

In many Muslim countries, women have few rights and must wear traditional Muslim clothing, including veils. In Egypt, however, women have more freedoms than the women living in other Muslim countries. Still, the Egyptian police often ignore cases in which women say their husbands are **abusive**.

This woman is working on the restoration of an Egyptian Jewish **synagogue**. There are very few synagogues in Egypt.

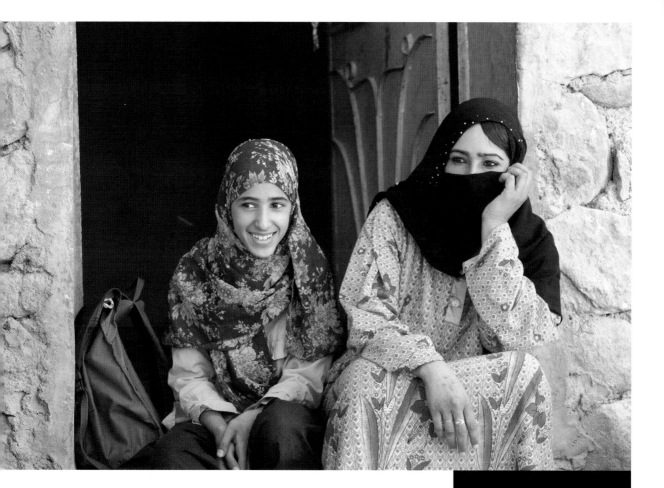

The Bedouins

A small but significant part of Egypt's population is **Bedouin**, an early group of Arabs who live in the desert. Many still live in traditional ways, in tents and travelling through deserts, but others have begun to settle in a single location – even in the larger cities. Traditional Bedouin men wear layered and flowing robes. They also wear cloths around their heads and necks as defense against the hot desert sun and wind. Women wear black dresses with head covers. Today, most Bedouin children wear modern clothing.

Many Bedouins are choosing to settle into modern life rather than live the traditional **nomadic** life.

Food in Egypt

Islam forbids eating pork, and cows are not generally kept in Egypt. Therefore, lamb and chicken are the most popular meats. Because of the Aswan **Dam**, fish have also become a popular source of protein.

Traditionally, Egyptians eat family dinners at home, but street vendors everywhere sell quick dishes such as *falafel*, or fried chickpea balls. Western-style fast food restaurants are now more popular and have changed the way people eat.

Egypt's market places are usually crowded with both tourists and locals. Markets specialize in items such as food or cloth.

Daily life

A typical Egyptian meal starts with a collection of small dishes, called *mezzes*. Choices might include *hummus*, a chickpea-based spread, or *tabbouleh*, a salad with cracked wheat, parsley, and tomatoes. The *mezzes* are often followed by a main course of mixed grilled meats or seafood – or vegetarian choices. Sweets such as *baklava*, made of nuts and honey, and other desserts made of grains and fruits are popular desserts in Egypt.

Cucumber and chickpea salad

Salads like this one are enjoyed around Egypt. Ask an adult to help you make this recipe.

Ingredients

- 2 tins chickpeas (also called garbanzo beans), drained
- 200 g tomatoes, chopped
- 1 large onion, chopped
- 2 sticks of celery, chopped
- 1 cucumber, chopped
- 2 teaspoons of minced garlic
- 1 teaspoon dill
- 3 teaspoons red wine vinegar
- 125 ml olive oil

Method

1. Mix oil and vinegar and set aside.
2. Combine all other ingredients, and then toss with the vinegar and oil mixture. Put the salad in the fridge for about an hour before serving.

Hollywood of the Arab world

Cairo is considered the Hollywood of the Arab world, turning out films that are popular worldwide. Cairo is also the heart of Egypt's television stations; however, Egyptians with satellite TVs watch broadcasts from around the world, including from Europe and the United States.

AHDAF SOUEIF (B.1950)

Although she writes primarily in English, Ahdaf Soueif is one of the best-known Egyptian authors. Soueif is an outspoken critic of Israel's policies toward Palestinians and also an activist for **gay rights**. She lives in both London and Cairo. Her most famous book is *The Map of Love* (1999).

Egyptian literature has a long history. In 1998 Naguib Mahfouz, pictured here, was the first Egyptian to win a Nobel Prize.

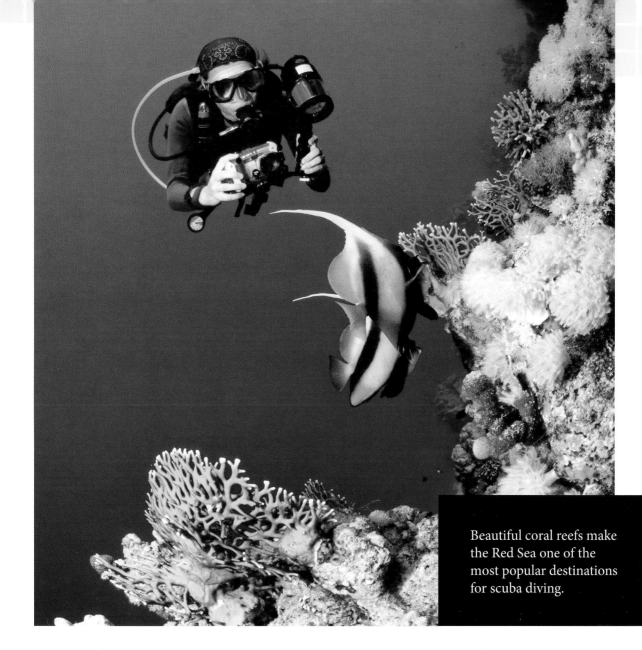

Beautiful coral reefs make the Red Sea one of the most popular destinations for scuba diving.

Sports

As in many Arabic and African countries, football is Egypt's most popular sport. When important matches are played, the country comes to a standstill. Other favourite sports include horse riding and racing. Water sports, such as water skiing, rowing, or sailing in traditional flat-bottomed boats known as *feluccas* are also popular in Egypt. The Red Sea is considered one of the best places in the world for scuba diving and snorkelling.

Egypt today

In 1869 Thomas Cook, one of the first travel agents, arranged a tour to Egypt. This was the beginning of modern tourism. While Egyptian oil and gas **exports** are significant, tourism is still Egypt's main source of income.

Depending on tourism is risky for any country, but it is especially risky for a country in the Middle East. In 2003, when the United States and its **allies** invaded Iraq, tourism in Egypt dropped dramatically. Islamic terrorists have also been known to target Egypt.

Although Egypt's political future is unclear, its place in history and its importance to the world is not. The beginnings of the culture of the modern world are rooted in Egypt. Its art, literature, and politics will continue to affect the entire world.

In 2011, Egyptians rallied against President Hosni Mubarak in Tahir Square in Cairo.

Despite many changes, Cairo continues to thrive as Egypt's largest city.

Fact file

Country name:	Arab Republic of Egypt
Capital:	Cairo
Language:	Arabic
Religions:	Muslim (90%), Coptic Christian (9%), Other (1%)
Type of government:	Republic; also considered a dictatorship
Independence date:	1953
National anthem:	Bilady, Bilady, Bilady ("My Homeland, My Homeland, My Homeland")

My homeland, my homeland, my homeland,
My love and my heart are for thee.
Egypt! O mother of all lands,
My hope and my ambition,
How can one count
The blessings of the Nile for mankind?

[Chorus:]
Egypt! Most precious jewel,
Shining on the brow of eternity!
O my homeland, be forever free,
Safe from every foe!

Population:	80,471,869 (est. 2010)
Life expectancy:	72.4 years (male: 69.5 years; female: 74.8 years)
Median age:	24 years (male: 23.8 years; female: 24.3 years)
Literacy rate:	74.3% (male: 83.4%, female: 65.3%)
Bordering countries:	Libya, Sudan, and the Gaza Strip
Total land area:	995,450 square kilometres (384, 345 square miles)

Largest cities:	Cairo (population 7,764,700)
	Alexandria (population 3,806,300)
	Giza (population 2,541,000)
Climate:	desert (hot, dry summers with moderate winters)
Major rivers:	Nile
Highest elevation:	Mount Catherine (Mount Sinai): 2,629 metres (8,625 feet)
Lowest elevation:	Qattara depression: -133 metres (-436 feet)
Currency:	Egyptian Pound (EGP)
Resources:	petroleum, natural gas, phosphates, iron ore, lead, zinc
Industries:	textiles, food processing, tourism, chemicals, pharmaceuticals, construction
Imports:	fuels, chemicals, foodstuffs, machinery equipment
Exports:	crude oil and petroleum products, cotton, textiles, chemicals

National holidays:

7 January	Coptic Christmas
25 January	National Police Day
25 April	Sinai Liberation Day
1 May	Labour Day
23 July	Revolution Day
6 October	Armed Forces Day

Famous Egyptians:

Amr Diab, singer (born 1961)
Euclid, father of geometry (300s BC)
Karam Gaber, athlete (born 1979)
Mohamed Al Fayed, businessman (born 1933)
Naguib Mahfouz, writer (1911–2006)
Omar Sharif, actor (born 1932)
Meriam George, model (born 1987)

Timeline

BC is short for "before Christ". BC is added after a date and means that the date occurred before the birth of Jesus Christ, for example, 450 BC.

AD is short for Anno Domini, which is Latin for "in the year of our Lord". AD is added before a date and means that the date occurred after the birth of Jesus Christ, for example, AD 720.

BC

3100	King Menes unites the kingdoms of Upper and Lower Egypt.
c. 2500	The pyramids of Gaza and the Sphinx are built.
525	Persians conquer Egypt.
30	Egypt becomes part of the **Roman Empire**.

AD

642	Muslim Arabs conquer Egypt.
1517	Ottoman Empire invades Egypt and rules for 300 years.
1798	**Napoleon Bonaparte** invades Egypt.
1799	Rosetta Stone is discovered.
1869	Suez Canal is finished.
1914	Egypt becomes a British **protectorate**.
1922	Egypt gains limited independence from Britain.
1952	Army officers led by Gamal Abder Nasser overthrow Egypt.
1953	Egypt is declared a **republic**.
1967	The Six-Day War occurs.
1970	Aswan High **Dam** is completed.
1978	Egypt's Anwar Sadat signs peace accord with Egypt.
1981	Sadat is **assassinated**; Hosni Mubarak becomes president.
2005	**Terrorist** bombing of Sharm el-Sheikh.
2005	Constitutional amendment allows multiple candidates to stand for president.
2011	Protests break out against economic conditions and President Mubarak **resigns**.

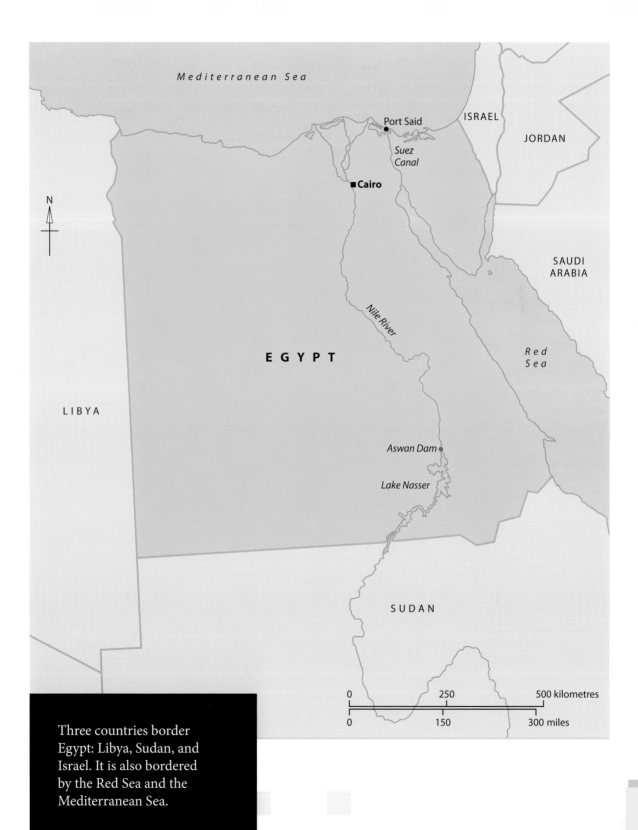

Mediterranean Sea

N

Port Said

Suez
Canal

■Cairo

Nile River

EGYPT

LIBYA

ISRAEL

JORDAN

SAUDI
ARABIA

Red
Sea

Aswan Dam

Lake Nasser

SUDAN

| 0 | | 250 | | 500 kilometres |
| 0 | | 150 | | 300 miles |

Three countries border
Egypt: Libya, Sudan, and
Israel. It is also bordered
by the Red Sea and the
Mediterranean Sea.

Glossary

abusive being cruel or violent to a person or animal

algae simple plants that don't have stems, roots, or leaves

ally friend

assassinate murder for political reasons

bank side of a river

Bedouin Arab of the desert in Asia or Africa

civilization culture and way of life of a certain group

colony country or territory ruled by an outside power or government

compulsory required by law

concession give something up, as in a compromise

dam something, usually a concrete structure, that holds back water in order to make electricity or to have a water supply

deposit natural accumulation of matter

dictator ruler with absolute power who often takes power by force

dictatorship form of government in which absolute power is held by a dictator

drought long period of little or no rainfall and the water shortage that results from it

dynasty family that rules a country and passes the power from one generation to the next

endangered at risk of becoming extinct

export something sold or sent to other countries

fertile (regarding land) capable of abundant plant growth

fundamentalism strict belief in a religion, often in its ancient form and ideology

gay rights equal opportunities for homosexual people

habitat natural environment for a living being

hieroglyphics ancient Egyptian form of writing that is made up of pictures and symbols

interim temporary; not lasting a long time

Islam religious faith of Muslims, based on the text of the Koran and teachings of the prophet Muhammad

literacy rate percentage of people who can read and write

Mamluk in Muslim societies, soldier that was a slave

migration mass movement from one place to another

mummify preserve a dead body by embalming and wrapping in cloth

Muslim follower of Islam, or having to do with a follower of Islam

Napoleon Bonaparte French emperor from 1804 to 1814 and for a short time in 1815

nomad person or group of people who intentionally move from place to place and who are without a permanent home

oases fertile areas in the middle of a desert

papyrus plant that grows along the banks of the Nile. Its leaves are used to make paper.

Pharaoh ruler in ancient Egypt

parliamentary democracy form of government in which people elect representatives who then choose a leader

peninsula narrow strip of land that sticks out into a sea or lake from a larger body of land

political party organization that wants to influence the government

protectorate country or area under the protection of another country, often following some of the other country's rules, but still maintaining independence in local issues

reform change something for the better

republic form of government in which the people elect their leaders

revere honour or worship

resign leave a job or position

revolution overthrow of a government by its people

riot noisy, violent public fight caused by a crowd of people

Roman Empire ruling power over much of Europe and Africa lasting from approximately 44 BC to AD 476

synagogue religious place for Jewish people

terrorism use of violence or threats to achieve a goal

translate change words from one language into another

Find out more

Books

Deserts (Geography Fact Files), Katie Powell (Ed) (Wayland, 2007)

Egypt (Countries of the World), Selina Wood (National Geographic, 2009)

Egypt (Enchantment of the World), Ann Heinrichs (Children's Press, 2006)

The Story of Islam (Usborne Young Reading: Series Three), Rob Lloyd Jones (E.D.C. Publishing, 2007)

Hosni Mubarak (Modern World Leaders), Susan Muaddi Darraj (Chelsea House, 2007)

Websites

www.bibalex.org/libraries/presentation/static/13513.aspx
Recapture the spirit of the ancient Library of Alexandria.

www.britannica.com/EBchecked/topic/180382/Egypt
Learn more about Egypt from the Encyclopedia Britannica.

http://kids.nationalgeographic.com/kids/places/find/egypt/
Country facts, information, stunning photos, and videos about Egypt can be found on this National Geographic website.

http://www.bbc.co.uk/learningzone/clips/living-near-the-river-nile/9023.html
Watch this BBC video clip about life on the river Nile.

Places to visit

If you are ever lucky enough to travel to Egypt, here are some wonderful places to visit:

The Great Pyramid of Giza

The largest and oldest pyramid, it was most likely built around 2,650 BC.

The Sphinx of Giza

The construction and meaning of this ancient statue remains a mystery.

Bedouin life

Tours can be arranged to see how modern Bedouins live.

The Red Sea

The Red Sea provides excellent snorkelling and scuba diving.

Topic tools

You can use these topic tools for your school projects. Trace the map on to a sheet of paper, using the thick black outline to guide you.

When Egypt achieved independence, many other Arab nations were also fighting for their independence from Britain. The red, white, and black colours are shared by Iraq, Syria, and Yemen and stand for the struggle. The golden eagle in the middle of the flag is the national symbol of Egypt.

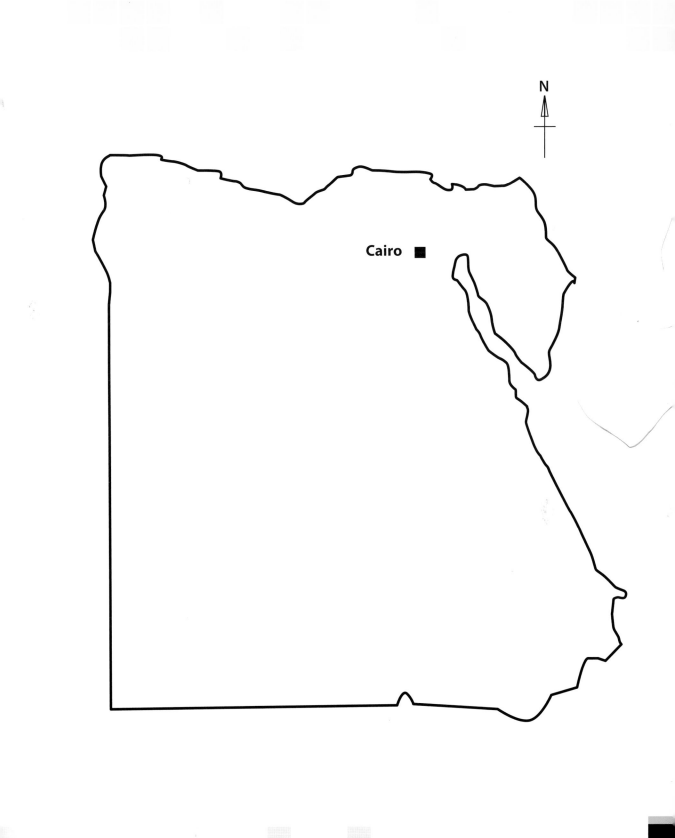

N

Cairo ■

Index

Titles in the series

Afghanistan	978 1 406 22778 9	Japan	978 1 406 23548 7
Algeria	978 1 406 23561 6	Latvia	978 1 406 22795 6
Australia	978 1 406 23533 3	Liberia	978 1 406 23563 0
Brazil	978 1 406 22785 7	Libya	978 1 406 23564 7
Canada	978 1 406 23534 0	Lithuania	978 1 406 22796 3
Chile	978 1 406 22786 4	Mexico	978 1 406 22790 1
China	978 1 406 23547 0	Morocco	978 1 406 23565 4
Costa Rica	978 1 406 22787 1	New Zealand	978 1 406 23536 4
Cuba	978 1 406 22788 8	North Korea	978 1 406 23549 4
Czech Republic	978 1 406 22792 5	Pakistan	978 1 406 22782 6
Egypt	978 1 406 23562 3	Philippines	978 1 406 23550 0
England	978 1 406 22799 4	Poland	978 1 406 22797 0
Estonia	978 1 406 22793 2	Portugal	978 1 406 23578 4
France	978 1 406 22800 7	Russia	978 1 406 23579 1
Germany	978 1 406 22801 4	Scotland	978 1 406 22803 8
Greece	978 1 406 23575 3	South Africa	978 1 406 23537 1
Haiti	978 1 406 22789 5	South Korea	978 1 406 23551 7
Hungary	978 1 406 22794 9	Spain	978 1 406 23580 7
Iceland	978 1 406 23576 0	Tunisia	978 1 406 23566 1
India	978 1 406 22779 6	United States of America	978 1 406 23538 8
Iran	978 1 406 22780 2	Vietnam	978 1 406 23552 4
Iraq	978 1 406 22781 9	Wales	978 1 406 22804 5
Ireland	978 1 406 23577 7	Yemen	978 1 406 22783 3
Israel	978 1 406 23535 7		
Italy	978 1 406 22802 1		